WHICH HOME IS FOR YOU?

The Basics You Should Know About Condo, HOA And Single Family Home

PATRICIA E. BASDEN

All rights reserved by Patricia E. Basden. This book or any portion thereof may not be reproduced or used in any manner whatsoever without the expressed written permission of the publisher except for the use of brief quotations in a book review.

ISBN: 978-0-578-39579-1

Published by:
www.PopPublishing.com
Atlanta, Ga. 30326

Table of Contents

Introduction 1

Chapter 1: Did You Realize? 6

Chapter 2: The Price May Be Right But… 9

Chapter 3: What Your Real Estate Agent, Title Company and Attorney Should Do for You 14

Chapter 4: Documents You Should Understand Before Buying in an Association 25

Chapter 5: The Background Approval Process 32

Chapter 6: Ways to Pay Your Fees 35

Chapter 7: Warranties You Should Know and Probably Purchase .. 40

Chapter 8: 40 Year Recertification 44

Chapter 9: Suggestions from Prior and Current Owners 48

Chapter 10: The Hysterical Side of Living in a Condo 55

Chapter 11: Gut Wrenching Questions 58

Chapter 12: The Necessity of Rules 61

Chapter 13: Breakdown of The Boards 63

Chapter 14: Maybe You'd Rather Buy a Home in an HOA 68

Chapter 15: Maybe You'd Prefer a Single Family Home 71

Chapter 16: Other Tips 73

Chapter 17: BONUS CHAPTER: Real Life Stories 81

Acknowledgements and Credits 87

Glossary 89

Introduction

I wrote this book to inform three groups: current homeowners, potential homeowners, and the younger generation, who are unaware of the purchasing process and the distinctions between moving into an association or into a single-family home. I aim to bring awareness to some of the steps you will take before you acquire one of these types of homes. I also mention that although you may be an owner in a homeowner's association, there are certain rights you will relinquish to the board members you elect.

I share different experiences that prior and current owners believe are in your best interest to know before you decide which type of home is right for you. I find it crucial to encourage anyone on the path to homeownership, especially young adults, to solicit professional help before making major financial decisions. There is a plethora of purchasing-related information you may be unaware of.

Additionally, there is a negative connotation about renting that is unwarranted. I reassure young adults in particular to not let society's expectations guide them, but instead, be empowered to make the decisions that suit them. As you read the information gathered from my experience, you will gain more insight into how to purchase and live in one of these homes.

I urge you, the prospective home buyer, to research and connect with a licensed realtor and mortgage lender to explore the best loan options for your unique circumstance. Whether renting or buying, it is essential to obtain and maintain a good credit score. The latter increases your chances of receiving better interest rates and association approval. However, this book isn't about financial literacy. Nor is it created to tell you ways to fix your credit. There are numerous books as well as credit repair agencies that teach you how to address those challenges. There are also first-time home buying classes for the taking, after you sift through the customer reviews.

Instead, my book shares details on purchasing a condominium, a home in an HOA, or a single-family home. I clarify the vital documents: the **Q&A**, Condo & HOA documents, **Rules and Regulations**, and the most important, the **Approved Budget**, to prevent you from buying a home you might not be mentally or financially ready to purchase. I beseech anyone interested in buying a home in an association to understand the **Approved Budget** document before choosing to purchase that property. This book also underscores that since your name is on the **warranty deed**, it's imperative to be involved in all the financial aspects of your home and not leave them to the realtor or the board of directors.

Furthermore, you will be given websites with information the realtor and title company will eventually discuss with you as their client. After all, you are paying a commission for their services, and are entitled to know your rights and their responsibilities toward you. As with the realtor, it does not fully serve you to leave certain decisions to them, as their primary aim is to make a commission. Since the purchase will

Introduction

be your investment, I advise you to be equipped to approach this process hands-on.

I have more than 12 years professional experience within two areas of the condo and HOA industry. I began by handling collection accounts for two different law firms in Florida. I left the law field to be directly employed in the condos and HOA industry as an administrative assistant, and later obtained my CAM or Community Association Management License to become an Assistant Property Manager.

Because I enjoy helping people, I felt it would be only right for me to disclose information to help others attain knowledge that is seldomly shared. I felt it essential to survey current and prior owners, especially those in associations and in **single-family homes.** When conducting these surveys, I asked them what they were unaware of before their purchase, and what they thought potential buyers should know before buying into an association. I believe advice from these groups will allow you to see the bigger picture and equip you to purchase that perfect home.

This is not to say that buying a home in an association is a horrible investment, or that I dislike associations. But as an Assistant Property Manager, I believe a book which offers an unbiased overview as this does is long overdue. I have not been in the field as long as other veterans have, but in my experience, most of them have yet to share the enclosed information with potential buyers in this way. I also present questions throughout the book with space for you to write your answers and to record the suggested information. The terms in bold letters are defined in the glossary at the back of the book. Being equipped with vital information will ease the journey toward your dream home.

My backstory

I started in the law field, not by accident, for I do not believe in coincidences. I will admit I had no intention of getting into law. While I was managing a custom clothier store in New York City, an attorney saw my negotiation skills and my passion for helping people in an honest way. How I finally decided to work for his law firm in Manhattan, New York, is for another book, as my intention is not to promote any firm, realtor, insurance company, or specific management company.

After a couple of years at his firm, I moved to Long Island, New York to a law firm in West Hempstead, where I assisted in the Personal Injury Trial and Medical Malpractice departments. I then relocated to Coconut Creek, Florida, where I was hired by a firm that handled collections for condominiums and HOAs. Between my tenure at these firms from 2009 to 2015 and being overwhelmed by my role in foreclosures and the growing numbers who lost their homes, I decided to work directly in the condominium management industry. I ventured in as an administrative assistant for a couple of years in the Condo division. After that, I eventually obtained my **LCAM** to become an Assistant Property Manager in South Florida.

Introduction

Purchasing this book is your first step to empowerment in the process of home ownership. I am sure the information I have chosen to disclose will help keep you on your toes. You can rely on this as well as your realtor's guidance, so that you do not buy a condominium or other type of home solely because the price seems right. Keep in mind I am not a lawyer. Therefore, checking with licensed legal counsel on the particulars for your state is always advised. Once you have read this from cover to cover, you will be able to make an informed decision before you purchase a home in good faith. However, I must warn you that you might reconsider the type of home you initially intended to purchase.

Chapter 1:
Did You Realize?

Before you decide which home style is right for you, let us look at the differences between a condominium, an HOA, and a single-family home. And then I will give an overview on purchasing a condominium.

Condominiums are typically individually owned units in a building. They may consist of a hundred and fifty units or more, where owners pay a certain percentage depending on the square footage of ownership. In addition, these owners must pay maintenance fees to cover the common area expenses and sometimes **special assessment**(s), to take care of a significant project the association's approved budget or reserves do not cover. This style of home is run independently or by a property management company.

HOA is a homeowner association which consists of homes built on a particular lot of land considered to be one community. The owners are responsible for paying a mortgage, a fee to maintain the common areas, and for complying with the rules the association has set in place. Property management companies usually run this association, or it is self-managed.

A single-family home is a stand-alone building where the owner pays the mortgage and maintains all aspects of the house. Although the condo and HOA have their rules and board members who run them, this home style has its set of rules and is given structure by the housing code enforcement.

You may believe purchasing a condo is the best home for you because:

- You do not have to maintain the lawn.
- It is in a gated community.
- You are excited that you do not have to go too far to exercise.
- You find the location of the condominium awesome because it is near family and shopping.
- You have access to a pool without having to personally maintain it.

But are you aware if you purchase a condo that...?

- You can only have a certain number of family and friends in your unit at one time. Please review the association condo documents.
- Most condominiums will not allow you to move in or out on the weekends. Please review the Rules and Regulations of the association.
- You may have one parking space, at most two, as opposed to having an **assigned parking** space. Inquire if the condo you intend to purchase comes with a **deeded parking space, do they accommodate electric vehicles (EVs).**

Inquiries you should make if you are an EV owner.

- How many charging stations are in the building, is there a fee, is this service provided on a first come first served basis. Does the association have the correct connector for your EV because there are several types, J1772, Type 1 and Type 2, you may need to purchase an adapter. Is the charging station self-serve or if an attendant is available 24/7 to assist when needed? Explore the option if the association permits owners to place charging stations at the parking space connected to the possible unit and if yes what are the requirements. Are the responses acceptable to you?

- The board of directors sets the approved budget and helps to make the final decisions that the property management company recommends they address.

- You will need to comply with all the rules the association has in place.

Don't be discouraged if after reading these facts you are rethinking the purchase of a condo. Some residents feel that some of these rules are made by board members who wish to exert control over them. But having these restrictions isn't entirely bad. On the bright side, some rules are created to protect your investment. After all, it will be your home and you will be considered an investor if you decide to purchase one. I do see the benefits if the rules and regulations are followed. By keeping most of them, the free-for-all mentality that often results in diminished property values, will be abolished in these communities.

Chapter 2:
The Price May Be Right But...

The first document that you should be aware of is the Q&A. The Q&A is a question-and-answer sheet that will give you an idea of what you should ask before attempting to purchase the condominium. Below is a sample of the questions typically found on a questionnaire that you should be able to answer:

- Is there a current special assessment in place?

    YES_____ or NO _____

- If there is a special assessment, how long is it for and when will it end?

- How much is the special assessment? _____

- Can the HOA supply a breakdown of what the special assessment is for?

- Did you receive it?

    YES_____ or NO _____

- Are there rental restrictions?

    _____

    _____

    _____

    _____

Which Home Is for You?

- How many **litigation cases** are active? _____

- Does the condominium come with a storage unit?

    YES_____ or NO _____

- What type of financing is allowed, 10% or 20%?

    _____

- Is **FHA** allowed?

    YES_____ or NO _____

- Is there a minimum down payment required?

    YES_____ or NO _____

- If the condominium has a balcony, who will own it, the association or you?

- Association _____ You _____

- What are the rules and regulations regarding pets, parking, and guests?

    _____

    _____

- Does the condominium have a current **wind mitigation**?

    YES_____ or NO _____

- Does the condominium have **flood insurance**?

    YES_____ or NO _____

These are questions you should have your realtor ask the seller's realtor:

- Did the seller leave the A/C unit on regularly?

    YES_____ or NO _____

- This question is important to ask in the state of Florida.

- Ask if the association has central A/C units. The answer can determine if there have been major problems with the unit you will inherit.

- Who maintained the A/C if it is included in the sale of the condominium?

- Company's name: _____

- If the A/C is a central unit, inquire how many times the filter should be changed.

- Were there mold issues prior to this potential sale?

    YES_____ or NO _____

- Did the seller add a room or change the **floor plan** of the condo with or without the permission of the association?

    YES_____ or NO _____

It's important to know this information, because as the new owner you could become responsible for fees that surface if floor plan alterations are discovered by the association. Whether the discovery is made by a 40-year recertification review of your unit, or by the engineer who has to go into the unit during an emergency, it's in your best interest to get the seller to state they have not changed the condo's footprint. If it is discovered they did, they will be responsible for any fees equated with this discovery. If the association approved the change, you need to inquire if the permit has been closed.

As a beginning step, look up the property appraiser's website. Once you type in the property's address under the property search, you will be shown the description of the number of beds/baths in the home. There are other details you should learn between the realtors and the property search:

- Do you see the number of rooms and bathrooms listed on the property appraisal?

- Is it the same number of rooms and bathrooms that are listed in the sales ad?

- How many rooms? _____ How many bathrooms? _____

- Did the seller have any plumbing issues?

    YES_____ or NO _____

- Does the association allow washers and dryers in the condo? (Even if you see one in the condo, ask).

    YES_____ or NO _____

- How old are the seller's windows? _____ If the windows are less than five months old, request that the seller provide you with the vendor and **warranty** information.

- Has the seller ever attended a board meeting?

  YES_____ or NO _____

- If yes, did they feel their concerns were heard and addressed?

- Does the association have rules against smoking in their condo or on their balcony, if there is one?

  YES_____ or NO _____

- What year was the building built? _____

- If the building is 40 years old, has it passed the 40-year recertification?

  YES_____ or NO _____

- Did you inquire if the building was properly maintained?

  YES_____ or NO _____

- One premium concern: is the condo considered capable of withstanding a possible hurricane or tornado?

I hope you have done your due diligence to find the answers to the questions listed above before you make an offer on that condo. Now that you have received your answers and if you still want to proceed with your purchase, awesome! Take a few more minutes to read the following chapters to become knowledgeable about what you must do regarding that purchase.

Chapter 3:

What Your Real Estate Agent, Title Company and Attorney Should Do for You

The Real Estate Agent

The next step over the next few weeks or months is to develop a working relationship with a real estate agent or two and with a title company. Additionally, an attorney must be involved to review all the documents that will pertain to this sale. You need to know his or her role in getting you your dream home. Procuring these professionals are necessary steps for any type of home you wish to buy.

As a potential home buyer, I hope you interview at least two agents to determine which one is best suited to assist you in this process. Speak with others around you who recently purchased their home and who would recommend their services. After all, buying a home isn't a one, two, three step process. This individual will become your advisor, and your unlicensed therapist when things don't go according to plan. It is always best to choose a real estate agent after the following inquiries:

- Always confirm the agent has a current license.
- In addition to your friend's referral, ask if the agent has other references with whom you can speak directly.

- Ask how many homes this real estate agent have has sold and in what areas.

- Ask if the real estate agent sells homes full-time or part-time.

- Ask how many clients the realtor has at the time you are considering engaging them. This may not seem important to you, but you will not want to work with a realtor who has four or more clients and does not have enough staff to assist them. WHY? Because your realtor is a human being, not a robot. They will still need to function appropriately within a limited amount of time.

- Ask for the best way to communicate with the agent.

Most importantly, it is imperative that you feel comfortable handing over your personal and financial information to this person. You will also have to share who you are and what your wishes are with them.

These are some of the duties a good real estate agent should perform in the insurance buying process:

- Get you connected with a trusted lender according to your financial status. Initiate the process for you to be **pre-approved**, whereupon you will provide your credit information, employment verification, additional income, etc. Inform you of the amount the lender requires, which will determine how much money you will need to purchase that condo, HOA, or single-family home.

- Explain to you that your **pre-qualified** loan amount is not a guaranteed amount of money you will receive. Your agent helps you to understand that the amount you are pre-approved for and can spend on your lovely home depends on your credit score and verified income.

- The agent will meet with you and listen to your wants and needs. Then give you suggestions as to the location(s) that fits your current financial capabilities and requirements.

- The real estate agent should guide you as to the true value of the home, then advise you on your first offering price. Also, the realtor can lead you in the event your first offer is not accepted.

- An agent should recommend a few reputable home inspection companies to obtain inspection reports. For Florida condos, your inspection report should include mold, lead paint, and possibly water. Due to the year-round temperatures, you must ensure mold hasn't formed anywhere in that home. If that home was built in 1978, you should have a lead report done. Also, inquire about the life expectancy of the pipes. Keep in mind *The Lender* is the person who orders the appraisal on a financing deal.

- A good agent will be present during the inspection or due diligence period. After all, you are paying that person a commission, according to your specific sales agreement. You should be there as well if you can. Once the report is completed, the realtor should discuss with you the repairs or

- replacements that are to be brought to the seller's attention. The realtor will suggest that you make a proposal to the seller to fix the issue(s) in exchange for a reduction in price.

- An experienced real estate agent should manage all of the expectations of the buyer during the sale process. Upon entering a Sales Agreement, this should be signed by both the buyer and the seller. All monetary transactions will be handled by the assigned escrow agent.

- During the home purchasing process, the real estate agent especially the lender, will remind the buyer NOT to buy big-ticket items, such as a car, open new credit cards or loans, as these may cause your credit score to drop. A lowered credit score can also affect your interest rate, along with your debt-to income ratio. These factors play a major part in how much of a loan you will qualify for.

- There is so much more a real estate agent should do for you, but these are the core services you can expect.

Title Company

The Title company plays a significant role when buying a home. They offer a range of services that can make the journey easier for you. They generally include:

- Finds out if there is a first right of refusal available to the members or the association. **The first right of refusal** is when the board/association has the right to purchase the property in question, before the seller can accept an offer from a buyer. Please review association documents.

- When doing their title search, the title company (possibly the in-house attorney) inquire about the ad valorem, (which means if there are taxes levied against the property) at a certain rate depending upon the property's value.

- Confirms there are no liens recorded from contractors who have done work or are currently doing work on the condo/HOA. There may be liens against the property you plan to purchase, which could remain in place for up to ten years or more if they are not resolved. This is when your title company acquires a **sufficient funds affidavit** from the association. This proves they have enough funds to complete the work the contractor has started.

- Investigates if the current seller has outstanding **violations** from the Association.

- Can set up the escrow account pertaining to the sale.

- Certifies you obtained insurance for your property. It dispenses vital information from the insurance company.

- Facilitates the closings and new account set up fees.

- Distributes the payments during the closings once the buyers and sellers have signed all required documents. They are also known as escrow holders.

- Records the Warranty Deed and Mortgage paperwork.

- Issues the title insurance policy which protects the lender against issues with their title to the property. If a lien is recorded during the process of buying your condo, and it was done *after* the title company did their lien search, the insurance warrants that the title company take the necessary steps to address the lien. (The title insurance does not cover termites or mold once you obtain a clear title to the condo homes).

- Verifies the seller is the true owner of the property before your closing. The title company orders an **Estoppel,** which is a document that states if the current owner has an outstanding **maintenance** or special assessment balance. This process can take up to ten to fifteen business days to be received. The Estoppel states:

    - The date of issuance and individual requesting the Estoppel.

    - The seller(s') name.

    - The address of the property being sold.

    - The parking space or garage space, if applicable.

    - Details concerning maintenance and special assessment.

    - If there is a right of first refusal provided to the members or the association. The **first right of refusal** is when the board/association has the right to purchase the property before the owner can accept an offer from another seller. Please review association documents.

- Closing information
- **Estimated Close Date.**
- If the current seller has violations outstanding from the association.
- New account set up fee.
- Insurance information such as the agent's company name, phone number, fax number, and email address.

At the time of this book, the maximum amount your title company can be charged for the Estoppel is $299.00. But if the seller's account is delinquent, meaning they are in collections, you can be required to pay an additional $150.00. The maximum amount that a title company can be charged for a rush fee in order to have information provided in 3 days instead of the 5-business day or longer period, is $119.00.

An Estoppel is only good for thirty days. It's important for you to know without a doubt that the Estoppel is current at the time of your closing if you decide to purchase in an association. This way, you are sure about the amount of maintenance you will need and if the home has a special assessment.

I must stress the importance of the Estoppel. If there isn't one, you, as the new buyer, will be responsible for the fees the prior owner accumulated and didn't pay. In the state of Florida, the association usually directs the title company to obtain the Estoppel from a third-party company like HomeWiseDocs. If the association is self-run, then it should either provide the document or inquire where to purchase one on your behalf. If the title company doesn't purchase the Estoppel, it can be held liable for not doing so as it is required at all closings. There is also a space on the Estoppel for the preparer to provide any comments vital to the condo in question.

It's always best to have your Estoppel include the fees of the upcoming months' maintenance to avoid any issues in your first month of purchase. Most condos provide coupon booklets, but sometimes there is a delay, and you don't receive your booklets on time. However, with or without the booklets, you will still be responsible for paying for your maintenance and a special assessment fee, if one is owed.

It's also important to note the grace period you have before you will acquire a late fee of $25.00 or whatever the association has set as the penalty for late payments. This is also to prevent your account from going to the collection attorney.

Your Attorney

It's recommended for the title company and, the real estate agent to be present for the closing; however, it's not mandatory for a real estate attorney to be involved. Although it's suggested for a real estate attorneys be involved in the closing process. It's always suggested for the buyer to pick a closing attorney or title company that is in-house for an extra pair of eyes. Since this lawyer is the one person who must communicate and coordinate with all the players in this process, you want someone who is approachable and accessible.

Some of the major duties a real estate lawyer performs are:

- Conducts the title search on the desired property, as they are qualified to access such information.

- Reviews the legality of all documents that pertain to the transaction and resolves land & tenant disputes.

- Prepares all closing documents and does what is necessary for the closing to take place on time.

- Forwards closing funds to the seller's lawyer to secure keys to the property.

The cost to retain an attorney could run you between $150.00 to $500.00 in Florida, as of this writing. This and other fees vary from state to state.

The Closing

Information and items you should know and have for a smooth closing:

- A photo ID

- A certified cashier's check/or wire instructions to send balance to closing agent/title company on the day of closing.

- A copy of the **purchase agreement**

- A copy of the condo insurance.

- It's best to request that your closing take place on a Monday through Thursday morning, or before Friday afternoon. Why? Because the afternoons can be more difficult to get the assistance you may need. On Fridays, workers are mentally looking forward to the weekend and being off. This forces you to wait until Monday to address any issues that arise.

The closing is attended by you, the seller, lawyers from both sides, the real estate agent, and title company representatives. When signing and initializing the closing documents, carefully review the documents to confirm that all parties' names are correctly spelled. Misspelled names can cause a delay in the closing for days or even weeks.

When the closing is over, you should walk away with a copy of the **Warranty Deed**. This confirms the seller legally owned the property with no outstanding **liens,** mortgages, or anything else against it. It also establishes that no outside party has a right to the property once you purchase it. This is very different from receiving a **Quitclaim Deed,** where the seller does not guarantee he or she owns the title to the property being sold to you. The original Warranty Deed document is kept with the lender until the mortgage is paid in full. Once the closing is done, you as the buyer, MUST provide the condo and/or the HOA Association with a copy of the Warranty Deed and **HUD** (Closing Statement).

Changing Your Mind

Finally, as per https://www.experian.com, the **right of rescission** is a legal right consumers have to cancel certain types of home loans, such as a refinance, home equity, home equity line of credit (HELOC), and even some reverse mortgages. It gives consumers three days to rescind an agreement and receive a refund. For prospective condo buyers who may purchase from a developer, Florida Law requires all buyers be provided with a 15-business day rescission period, according to https://www.lawfirmnaples.com. This period begins once the buyer has signed an acknowledgment form that they are in receipt of all condominium documents. Rescission varies when it comes to different homes. Therefore, I encourage anyone who is in the process of a home purchase to ask the realtor the legal period of time when they may withdraw it. This will differ from state to state.

Chapter 4:

Documents You Should Understand Before Buying in an Association

Documents You Are Beseeched To Read and Understand...
Declaration of the Condominium

This document carries the most weight of any other document: This document

- Advises owners of their responsibilities.
- Outlines the responsibilities of the condo association.
- Describes the **common elements** and how they are shared.
- Discloses the unit owner's voting rights.
- Discloses the insurance requirements of the owners and the association.
- Discloses the process of conducting board meetings and voting.

  ALL ASSOCIATIONS have their individual declaration.

  Please keep in mind that rule(s) stated in the declaration generally are not subject to change. However, if more than a certain percentage of owners agree to alter a rule, it can be done. I know of a condo community where several owners requested a change to the number of years of ownership that was required before they could rent.

The documents restricted an owner from renting within the first two years of ownership. The documents also stated that a 75% homeowner agreement was required in order for the rules to be adjusted. Since numerous owners were against the policy, voting proxies were mailed out. 75% of the owners submitted to changing the number of years from two years to one and the rule was successfully changed.

By-laws

This document advises on:

- The manner in which the BOD (board of directors) meetings are called.
- The length of meetings.
- How notices are to be done and posted.
- Procedures for amending the bylaws.
- How the board of directors administers policies regarding the bylaws.
- How to oversee the maintenance and administration of the association.

Notice Of Intent to Sell by Owner

Most, if not the majority of condominium associations, need you to complete this document before they consider your application. It requires:

- The names of the buyer and seller.
- The unit number.
- For the seller to provide a copy of the sales contract.
- A copy of the seller's current recorded deed.
- For the seller to provide the buyer(s) with the most recent edit of the condo documents and updated Rules and Regulations for the buyer to sign and notarize.

Certificate Of Approval

This document is critical in order for your closing to take place. It only has a few lines, but it states the association's approval of the buyer to purchase in its community and to become one of its members. This is a notarized document.

Once you submit all the pre-ownership documents, please keep in mind some associations take up to 30 days to review and approve your purchase. There is no need to have your realtor call the association 1 or 2 days after your submission to inquire about the status of the application. They will contact you if there is a problem. Remember, you need to have a Certificate of Approval to close your deal.

Approved Budget

As a soon-to-be owner of a home or a condo in an association, you should understand the approved budget. It is a projection of the funds the association needs to cover its operating expenses. It also gives you an idea of the estimated expenses you will be responsible for by owning in that association. <u>It is crucial to obtain a receipt</u> when you receive the above documents and the approved budget. This is because you have a certain number of days to review and cancel the contract, if you DO NOT believe this major purchase is for you.

Categories in most condominium budgets that your maintenance will or should cover:

- Payroll of the employees of the condominium.
- Contracts: security services, pool services, lights, exterminator service, landscaping, elevator service, housekeeping.
- Insurance for the common area/ building(s).
- Utilities: water & sewer, trash.
- Wi-Fi and other amenities that may vary by location.

Basic maintenance usually consists of landscaping, trash removal, and possibly Internet and Wi-Fi, although some services and amenities vary. Compare the old budget to the newly approved budget and note if the board of directors has factored in salary increases, and supplies / items needed to maintain the property.

The BODs have a fiduciary responsibility to increase necessary maintenance by 15% without the association owners' vote. As an owner, you have the right to see the monthly financials. They are usually a month behind and will be posted on the association's website if the condo consists of 150 units or more.

Reserve Budget

There are crucial details in the approved budget you need to fully understand like the Reserved Budget breakdown. Inquire if the association has fully funded reserves at a healthy 70% - 100%. This will outline the amount reserved for repair and replacement projects costing $10,000.00 or more. Depending on the condominiums, the following items in the common areas will eventually need to be refurbished or replaced: mailboxes, elevators, balcony enclosures and exterior, fitness and pool (resurface/deck), and garage/parking. You will also need to replace the furniture and heater(s). Also find out if there are any major plumbing reports associated with the communal areas, because this may signal that the pipes need to be changed and require a future special assessment.

Other major projects related to roofing, pavement, and restoration stucco, are high-priced and require the association to save for over a period of time. This period is usually ten years, based on the warranty. Generally, the materials are chosen by the developer, or as the board of directors sees the need for a job.

You may want to find out if the association has done a recent Reserve Study.

A **Reserve Study** is a budget planning tool that observes the funds collected to date for the items in question. A funding plan is then put into place to offset the ongoing items.

Owners have brought to my attention that if a condo and/or home association has NO reserves or only a small one, owners will eventually have to pay a large special assessment. They say no matter how great the sale price is, the potential buyer should RUN from this investment. If a potential owner still wishes to buy, they should have at least $5K- $10K or more set aside as part of their personal reserves for emergency expenses.

Do NOT think if you buy a condo or a home in an HOA the low maintenance price will stay that way forever. All maintenance fees will increase. There is no way to get around this.

There are other categories you should read closely to know if the fees have increased or have been collected at all. They are covered under **Revenue** which includes income from parking, laundry, pet fees, fob/key card, and rentals. These rentals can include a unit acquired by foreclosure and for which the association obtained the title. This should state if the association acquired a foreclosed unit (usually for nonpayment of maintenance fees) with a mortgage on it, and if they are renting it to recoup the money. This category demands that you pay close attention to the flow of funds.

Therefore, once you become an owner/investor, review your monthly financial statements. Don't wait until you realize areas are in disrepair to start asking questions. Attend board meetings. During the health and wellness of the community segment designated for owners' questions, present your concerns. However, if your issue pertains to the topic on the agenda for that night, ask it at that time.

Purchase Agreement

Is a contract between the buyer and seller which outlines the details of the sale of the property:

The agreement lists and explains the following:

- The terms of the sale and what is included.
- What must take place before you obtain the condo.
- What will happen if the sale does not take place.
- The date of the closing.
- The default provisions or what will occur if one party doesn't live up to the agreement.
- Who pays for the property inspections, and what will follow if any deficiencies are uncovered.
- When you can take possession of the home after the closing.

Chapter 5:
The Background Approval Process

It is key that you are clear about the approval process & the fees required when you purchase a home in an association. Know that associations have a right to charge individuals 18 years and older $100.00 - $150.00 per application for an approval process to take place. Married couples are charged one price but must also submit a marriage certificate with the application. In addition, all applicants will be asked to give the association the authority to pull their credit and criminal histories.

Remember, the board of directors are volunteers. It may take up to 30 days for them to make a decision on your application considering the number of applications they must review. If an association does not provide you with a decision by the 30th day, your application is considered automatically approved by law. Check with your state for the amount of time your application becomes automatically approved if a decision is not made in a timely manner.

Some associations offer a rush fee to guarantee a decision under thirty days. You can ask the management office before you proceed with your submission if they provide this service. The condominium association will ask you to complete or present the documents below in no particular order:

The Background Approval Process

- A marriage certificate if you are married.

- A specific number of paystubs determined by the association.

- Tax Returns and W-2 forms determined by the association.

- Color copy of your ID. When you submit your ID to the company processing your application, they are required to blackout the license number and your DOB.

- A copy of your vehicle(s) insurance and registration if you will be parking your vehicle on the property.

- Pictures of your vehicle(s) to be parked on the property.

- A copy of your passport if you are a non-U.S. resident. Once again, the background company will blackout the passport number for your safety before releasing your information.

- A specified number of bank statements.

- Pages you will either sign or initial that you have read your rules and regulations.

- Proof of pet vaccination /veterinary records. First check whether the association allows pets and how many, before you pay to have your documents reviewed. You may need a letter from your health professional to certify that your pet is an emotional support animal along with a picture of your pet. You do not pay to register **ESA** emotional animals.

- A form which asks if you are active in the military or self-employed. If your answer is yes to either or both, you may need to present proof that you can sustain the fees related to ownership.

- A list of occupants eighteen and older who will reside in the unit. Depending on the association, a background check on all individuals may be mandated. You can inquire if a police background check is sufficient for the young adult(s) if they will not be responsible for condo fees.

- Inquire about move-in and delivery fees for appliances and security deposits. Each association has its set fees which can be refunded in agreement with the Rules & Regulations.

The forms of payment used to issue refunded deposits are personal and cashier's checks and money orders if no damage has been done to the property during the move-in. Please remember that if you give a personal check to **reserve** the elevator or for use of an amenity, you must verify with your state how long that check will be considered valid.

- Inquire about the fee for the Architectural packet if you intend to work on your unit before you occupy. This payment is REFUNDABLE

- Inquire about the Administrative Fee.

Chapter 6:
Ways to Pay Your Fees

This chapter will enlighten you on ways to pay your monthly maintenance and/or special assessment fees. It will also inform you about the ways to prevent your account from going into **Collections**, and the subsequent costly attorney fees. It is important for you to choose the best payment option to avoid delinquency.

Disclaimer: I am not an attorney. If you intend to rent your condo, I strongly suggest you read 718.116 (11) Florida Statutes on renting your unit. Please still do further research to determine if the same rules apply to your state. Also, check the association's rules and governance regarding tenant rights. If you are renting out your condo, confirm if your tenants will still be allowed to use amenities and have continued access to association property, should your account go into collections. In some states, if you have a tenant in your unit and you have an outstanding balance, the association has the right to collect your tenant's rent in order to cover your fees until your account is current.

Most condominiums provide coupon booklets with twelve coupons for each month's payment. The coupons detail the owner's name, condo unit number, payer's ID number, serial number, the amount of either the maintenance and/or special assessment fee, and the address where the payment should be remitted.

When you remit your payments by standard mail, your personal or cashier's check, money order, along with your coupons to the noted address, may be delayed. If you submit your payment too late in the month, your best option is to use the next day or two-day postal option. Your payment may not be received for five to seven days before it is accounted for and cashed. I suggest you mail your payments, along with the coupon for the month you are paying, either on the 1st, 3rd or 4th of the month. This is to avoid late fees. If your rules state that late fees are applied on the 10th of each month, then your payment(s) need(s) to be received **before** the 10th.

As an owner, if you choose to set up a bank draft directly with your bank to pay your monthly maintenance and/or special assessment fees, your bank will simply issue a check and mail it to the address for remittance. Your maintenance will not be immediately paid and posted to the association on that date. It is not a wire transfer.

Most condominiums also allow owners to set up their accounts with automatic payments. It's crucial to note that if you use the **ACH-Automated Clearing House** payment option, you must confirm and not assume your account has a zero-dollar balance. Owners typically set up their ACH to only pay the monthly maintenance amounts. If you set up ACH payments with an open balance (outstanding money amount down to two cents), and the ACH draft is only for the monthly fee that you have indicated on the ACH form, then your account will be delinquent each month until the open balance is paid off.

Some condominiums allow their owners to drop off payments to the management office. If you want to do this, please bring the coupon for that month with you so the staff member can confirm the correct payment amount. You should also request a stamped receipt for your records and scan it if possible. In the event management has made a human error and you can submit proof of payment, the association and/or the collection attorney is obligated to correct the amount proven to be reflected on the account ledger. They must also waive any late fees you were charged because of their accounting error.

Many condominiums allow payments by ClickPay, to the delight of owners. This is one of the ways to stay current and to avoid your account going to Collections. However, even with ClickPay, you still need to ensure your account has a zero balance before you set up this service. If you set up just the monthly amount with an open balance, your account will eventually become delinquent if the open balance is not paid first.

To prevent this, set up the option to "Pay All." It will draft whatever amount is owed on the account, including the open balance, so your account has a zero balance and is current at the end of every month. With ClickPay, you can be assured that only the amount owed on the account will be drafted. The system is programmed to know exactly what is owed on the ledger. Another almost perfect way to address your monthly maintenance fees and/or possible special assessment fee is to pay both fees in full.

It's also important for an owner to be aware of the maintenance fee changes. Budget meetings typically occur closer to the end of the year. Once the budget is approved, the January 1st maintenance fee may be different from the December's of the previous year. The association will have arranged for notifications to be sent to all owners regarding these budget changes.

You will then receive an updated coupon booklet with the new amounts. If you are an owner who pays your fees two or three weeks in advance, please follow up with the accounts management department to cover the balance owed for January because of the increased amount. It is important to note that if you have a ClickPay **Auto Pay** set up to "Pay All," ClickPay will automatically draft the new maintenance and special assessment fees amount each January. This takes the worry out of becoming delinquent each January if the amounts change.

Not all associations use ClickPay, but you can request that your board of directors investigate if this service can be available to the owners. This payment option accepts credit cards, checks, and ACH transfers, which owners find to be more convenient to make their payments. You will need to confirm the best method to make your payments on time. I trust this information will help you keep your account current and away from foreclosure. Also validate your mailing and email addresses, as well as phone number(s) are correct, and that you update them yearly and in-person with the association. I have heard owners complain about missed updates and communications concerning their property and accounts, only to discover their contact information was out of date.

The association is NOT RESPONSIBLE when an owner fails to communicate changes to their contact information after the first time they apply and are approved. When your information is updated with the association, there is less of a chance you not receiving all important notifications.

Chapter 7:
Warranties You Should Know and Probably Purchase

What You Should Have In Addition To the Four Walls...

You will have these major appliances in every home type you choose, so be familiar with their warranties. This chapter will offer suggestions on how to maintain these appliances for as long as possible.

You will want to keep your starting and ending date for each appliance handy (a space has been provided at the end of the book to record these dates). When you are purchasing that home and the appliance(s) appear to be new, ask the seller about the warranties they offer for those appliances. When you investigate, you will learn if a warranty transfer can take place within ninety days of the transfer of ownership.

The following appliances you should have a warranty for are:

Water Heater

- Water heaters are pricey; therefore, it is crucial to maintain this appliance. HOW? You should flush it at least every six months or so. But if you have extremely hard water or depending on the mineral content of your local water supply, you may want to flush it more often. You can purchase a water test kit at your local hardware store.

Air Conditioner

- Your air conditioner needs attention if you want a long life out of it. The maintenance process varies, but it is suggested that the appliance be maintained once a year. As for the filters, they should be changed every thirty days depending on the fiberglass filter you purchase. Some higher quality fiberglass requires changing twice a year. The higher the quality, the higher the price. Ask the property management company for a list of A/C companies who regularly maintain the condo or HOA units. The management company maintenance may offer this service for a fee. In your single-family home, ask the seller for that information. It's also wise to have your neighbors recommend a licensed A/C technician for those related needs.

Windows

- You are probably wondering how to maintain your windows. Well, there are a few measures you can take. Check your closed windows once every few months for drafts. Also look and feel if any water is seeping in due to a cracked or worn sealant. Being aware of these issues before your warranty ends is priceless.

If you discover air or water seeping in, contact the company that installed the windows to find out if they can provide you with an official observation. This will advise you if the cause is due to a crack in the foundation, or if your sealant simply needs re-caulking. Of course, this is after you've read your condo documents to clarify who is responsible for the windows in your unit.

If the windows are old and you don't have a warranty, or if the company has gone out of business, ask the management office for a list of approved vendors who have recently installed at that condo. Getting recommendations from your neighbors about their installers is a good idea as well.

Stove

- Warranties for stoves are usually one year in length. Therefore, inquire about the maintenance programs your appliance will qualify for after that year. In addition, if you are a buyer who prefers a gas stove because you're worried about power outages, check with the association about having one installed in your unit.

Dishwasher

- Dishwashers also usually have one-year warranties. However, www.consumerreports.org states that they have an average lifespan of six to ten years. You can purchase a home warranty and include this appliance.

Shutters

- If you purchase shutters for protection from the weather, privacy, and/or for aesthetic purposes, they should be maintained to keep or extend their lifespan, of 10 to possibly 30 years, depending on their material. This is according to the National Association of Home Builders/Bank of America Home Equity. Because of the wear and tear the weather will inflict on the exterior of your home, have your warranty information readily available. In my opinion, you should have your shutters cleaned and maintained at least once or twice a year as part of their upkeep.

Chapter 8:
40 Year Recertification

The information below is a combination of my experience assisting in three condo re-certifications and my research on the topic. I urge you to investigate the steps your condominium has taken to prepare for its 40-year recertification, so it is not deemed unsafe.

As part of your research in choosing a condo in Florida or any other state, you should know how long the condo was built before you purchase it. If it is forty years or older, find out if the building passed its forty-year recertification inspection and has been deemed safe for another ten years. According to the standards of the county/building code, a condo must be recertified for electrical and structural safety every decade.

Once the condominium receives the notice of recertification, they have ninety days to schedule the inspection. Should the inspection reports indicate that work needs to be done, the condo is given 60 more days to complete it. The inspection and repairs must be completed because the condominium then risks being deemed unsafe and could subsequently be evacuated, shut, or even torn down.

As an owner/investor, you should always cooperate with the scheduled building inspections. When owners don't comply or when the board fails to get the inspection done in a timely manner, the association incurs a $500.00 fee for the extension to be approved. Once the necessary repairs are outlined, the association will need to submit work permits which may be for electrical, structural, and illumination letters.

Electrical entails:

- To be done by a state registered professional engineer or architect with an active license.

- The licensed expert measures the level of illumination in the parking lot.

- Parking lot lighting illumination letter meets the maximum or minimum foot-candle per square foot.

Structural 5-page form entails:

- The date the inspection was started and finished.

- Description and condition of the structure, confirming the alignment condition.

- Supporting pictures of the items that need to be addressed.

- Masonry bearing wall or the condition of the wall carrying the load of floors and roof, in addition to its own weight.

- Floor and roof system consists of water tanks, air conditioning equipment, and cooling towers. It includes drains, scupper and conditioning towers, air conditioning.

- Steel framing system consists of the condition of exposed steel, elevator sheave beams, & connections and machine floor beams.

- Concrete framing system.
- Windows consisting of: fasteners and latches—the sealant inside and outside of the windows.
- Wood framing consists of metal fittings, drainage, and ventilation.
- Concrete restoration & waterproofing.
- Issues that cause concrete restoration related to buildings exposed to sea air and salt.
- Corrosion of reinforcing steel.
- Climate and pollution.
- Lack of adequate waterproofing material on the concrete and structure.
- Stress that is generated within the structure itself.

If these matters are not addressed regularly, they can result in significant financial problems and even become life safety issues as outlined in the DSSCONDO- *Development Services Solutions Condo* (a leading project management firm). If you purchase a condominium under 30 years old, verify that the board of directors and management with maintenance staff, regularly maintain the following areas to avoid issues that can arise at the 40-year certification.

- Mechanical equipment.
- Plumbing in common areas.

- Painting on a regular basis.
- Flooring repair in common areas.
- Electrical repairs such as light switches and exit signs in common areas. Heating and A/C systems for those areas.

Essentially, there should be preventive maintenance that is done on a regular basis with documentation of such maintenance readily available for the owners' review.

Chapter 9:
Suggestions from Prior and Current Owners

This chapter shares feedback from 12 current and prior owners who owned their condo for five to forty-five years. Each group was presented with seven questions and given an opportunity to make recommendations based on their experiences. Before the questions were presented to this group, I assured them I would not disclose their identities or the association they invested in. This section is for potential condo buyers, current condo owners, realtors, and title companies, who will find the enclosed information valuable to pass on to their clients. Several responses cover more than one topic. Therefore, it was not necessary to restate each question and answer here.

Our respondents were asked:

1. What year did you purchase your condo and when did you sell it?
2. Why were you interested in buying a condo?
3. What do you think a potential buyer should take into consideration before buying a condo?
4. Why did you sell your condo?
5. What do you wish you knew before buying your condo?

Suggestions from Prior and Current Owners

6. Would you buy another condo? If yes, why? If no, why not?

7. Is there anything else you want to say about condo ownership that I haven't asked?

I have summarized the findings to allow you to draw your own conclusions. I have included the most important excerpts from our discussion. Three respondents were repeat condo owners who purchased and lived in at least 2 different communities. A few were also purchased as investment properties as well as for their personal residence.

The overall pros that lead to ownership were:

- A favorable price in comparison to single-family ownership - Respondents #1,3,4,5,6,8,
- Proximity of amenities - Respondents # 2
- Lovely grounds and location in relation to job proximity and other personal considerations - Respondents # 8
- Maintaining a condo is less work than maintaining a house - Respondents # 4
- Security, guaranteed parking - Respondents # 3
- Living in a community where there is a low renter vs. high owner ratio -Respondents # 3

In their words:

- *"I chose to purchase a condo instead of a home because I travel, and I felt my home on its own would be vulnerable to break-ins. I felt an association with security would be safer."* Respondents # 4

- *"The price was great and the distance to work was perfect. It was exceptionally clean, and I liked the gated community with security. There were very few renters, which made the place cleaner since the owners cared about their properties."* Respondents # 3

- *"My reason for buying was the green space, the location of my unit across from the pool and the location of the property across the river from the park. No matter what I found out after purchasing my unit, my reason for buying would not change. The crappy board, uncaring unit owners, or pending assessment are temporary, and do not change my reason for buying."* Respondent # 1

The negatives that led to the decision to sell or to purchase only for investment were:

- Too many rules and regulations changes - Respondents # 6

- No authority over neighbors' behavior, especially renters - Respondent # 1

- Cost of assessments - Respondents # 2

- The board of directors' lack of knowledge to lead a business; dishonesty (in some cases), disregard for community's interest and inability to agree on critical issues. - Respondents # 8

- Poor financial health of condo (little or no reserves) - Respondents # 5

- Serious decisions are often left to those on the board with their own personal agendas that are not in line with the common good of the association and the owner majority. - Respondent # 1

- The overall feeling of a lack of control over something I was supposed to "own." - Respondent # 1

In their words:

– *"I did not know I had so few rights, being an apartment dweller for most of my adult life. For instance, it was like a punch in the gut to find out how many rules there were for visitors to see me. So much protocol and time-consuming red tape involved just to have an outside maintenance person come to look at my unit. Not to mention everything that is involved with having someone do actual work." - Respondent # 1*

– *"With my first condo, I only had an issue when they changed the rules while I was living there. No more pets were going to be allowed and my daughter had asked Santa for a cat." - Respondents (2)*

In response to what owners wish they knew going into the purchase:

- "I would have chosen a condominium that was more upgraded: better plumbing, updated fixtures, equipped with washers and dryers, and more pet friendly. I would've found out if the Board of Directors were able to make unified decisions. If the BOD doesn't come together; nothing gets done." Respondent #1

- "With my second condo, I wish I'd known it was going to be run like a communist country with NO ONE to help us. This included senators, detectives, and police." - Respondents# 2

In response to the question about advice for those who are considering a condo purchase:

- "I believe potential condo owners should take the time to review the financials, research the property management company, and check the association's rules and regulations. They need to inquire about the special assessment, request a copy of all the permits such as the 40-year recertification, the fire department inspection, and if there are any legal issues, etc." - Respondent # 2

- "I would buy another condo if the property were financially healthy and beautiful inside and out. I would need to see if the owners and the front office are taking care of it, if it is safe, under twenty years old, and if the property is upscale. This would be my recommendation for new buyers." - Respondent #1

Suggestions from Prior and Current Owners

- "I would count how many single individuals, younger people, or multi families were residing at the property. - Respondents # 6"

- "Do not buy. Only rent. A condo owner doesn't have control of their unit." - Respondent #1

- "I would urge the potential buyer to find out if there are any lawsuits pending against the condo association. Also, to find out how many rentals there are and if there have been any structural studies recently done on the building." - Respondent #1

- "Owners should pay attention to what is going on at board meetings and the projects that are being worked on. Unit owners who are not holding up their responsibilities will greatly affect how projects in the building and community get done. We had to pay an additional assessment for work that was improperly done after we paid the assessment for it to be done in the first place. The BOD should be transparent and not corrupt." - Respondents # 6

- "Inquire about mold, especially in Florida." - Respondents #5

- "I would tell them to first check with the local police to see the type of reports, like car theft, domestic violence, and gang activity the residents of the condominium are making." - Respondents # 2

Even though there were dislikes about the ownership experience, a few of the respondents would do it again, but with caveats:

- *"Yes, I think it is a good investment and it doesn't require much maintenance on my part. However, educating myself on the condo's finances is a factor." - Respondent #1*

- *"I am hesitant to say "yes," but the only reason I may consider buying another condo would be as an investment property." - Respondent # 1*

- *"I would if the price was right, and the financials mentioned above looked good." - Respondent # 1*

Given everything I hope you have learned up to this point, what do YOU think?

Chapter 10:
The Hysterical Side of Living in a Condo

I hope as a potential owner or current owner of a home in an association, you can remember that management is made up of human beings who don't need to be reminded that you pay a percentage of their salaries, whenever you feel things aren't going your way. Most of the time they are following the rules and regulations you agreed upon before buying into that association. I believe in professional customer service as well as courtesy and respect from all who are part of the condo living experience. I want to give you a perspective of the daily matters management addresses that cause us to say, WE CAN'T MAKE THIS STUFF UP!

- An owner called the office to request that we make the birds stop singing in the tree by her window in the morning.

- An owner came to the office to complain that their neighbor's unit required extermination because of roach infestation. When maintenance checked out both units, it was discovered the complainant was a hoarder.

- An owner emailed a picture of ducks taking dumps by her door in the morning as part of her request that they make the ducks eliminate *after* she left for work.

- An owner indicated they had a cousin who was staying with them "slightly" over the time limit the association allowed.

When I called to confirm the relationship with the owner, the individual stated they weren't related, but that s/he was leasing the unit for $1,200 per month. When I confronted the owner, they countered that the person didn't understand English. This was untrue because I asked the question in different ways to be certain I was understood.

- An owner called to report their upstairs neighbors copulated at certain times of the day. They believed the owners probably redid their floors without the correct soundproofing and they wanted management to ask them to lessen their frequency.

- A particular owner came to the office to complain about another owner's barking dog. It was discovered that the one who cited the violation had numerous pets in their own unit.

- A married owner wanted security to call the number on file whenever their significant other came to the front gate. The owner was having an extramarital affair and didn't want the two to meet at the home.

- A tenant attempted to register a new pet on a lease in which the owner indicated no pets would be allowed during the 12-month rental. Management was forced to contact the owner to determine if they had changed their lease conditions.

- An illegal tenant moved into a unit in the process of foreclosure. The tenant, who had been living rent free for several months, called management to ask why the association didn't send someone personally to inform them of the scheduled eviction. The previous owner had the illegal tenant "apply" to live in his unit, which gave us the information to begin eviction proceedings.

- An owner's boyfriend called the management office to say he saw ducks swimming in the pool before he went in it, and that he believed this caused his subsequent ear infection.

- An owner came to the management office and wanted to be reimbursed for the $35.00 package of butter the exterminator who serviced his unit had touched. When asked to present a receipt, he stated he didn't need to provide one.

Chapter 11:
Gut Wrenching Questions

These questions force you to be honest with yourself. If you answer YES to most of them, I promise you will regret buying a condo or into a HOA. If you do not have $5K-$10K (or more based on your state) set aside for emergencies, and to keep up with the increase in maintenance fees, or if you do not have the patience to conform to community life, then buying a home in an association may not be the best purchase for you.

- Are you on a fixed income?

    YES_____ or NO _____

    Maintenance will always increase with the chance that a Special Assessment will be passed.

- Do you have a large family?

    YES_____ or NO _____

- If your family intends to stay with you for more than a specific amount of time, they will be required to comply with all resident rules, including a background check.

- Do you get frustrated when someone tells you what you can and cannot do? You will have to provide the license and insurance for all vendors you contract to service your unit even with an emergency repair.

- Are you a smoker?

    YES_____ or NO _____

    If you are a smoker, you need to inquire if and where you can smoke. Also inquire if there are rules that protect you from other neighbors' smoke.

- Do you understand how much of your privacy you will give up when you move into a condominium, and are you okay with that?

    YES_____ or NO _____

- Do you have more than one vehicle?

    YES_____ or NO _____

- Do you have a commercial vehicle?

    YES_____ or NO _____

- Do you have a large truck?

    YES_____ or NO _____

- Associations have guidelines about the size and number of vehicles, so check if they are acceptable to you. If your children are about to become drivers, and will want their own car, the association may have policies to prevent that.

- Be prepared for the **Percentage Rule**. If you do not wish that a particular design of the condo be altered, but a percentage of the owners (as specified by the board) do, you will have to comply with the decision of that percentage whether you agree with them or not.

- Know the rules for pets. Do they suit you?

    YES_____ or NO _____

- Your guest(s) won't be able to visit you at your condo with their dog(s). Are you fine with that rule?

    YES_____ or NO _____

Chapter 12:

The Necessity of Rules

How Owners' Actions Can Affect Not Only Their Property Value But...

Many responsibilities come with condo, HOA, and single-family home ownership. However, these responsibilities are manageable if you can accept the actions needed to preserve the value of your property and that of your neighbors. Please keep in mind all homes come with rules you should abide by to avoid conflicts with your neighbors, the board of directors in your association, or with the Code Enforcement of your city.

You may have purchased a single-family home, but you cannot add an additional room to it without pulling the appropriate permits. Nor can you decide not to fix the roof or the windows, or to park non-working cars in the front yard. A **Noise Ordinance** prevents you from blasting music all hours of the night and Code Enforcement will not permit you to leave the grass uncut for extended periods of time. These are only a few of the actions in and outside your home that can affect the property value of the neighborhood. And when that time comes, selling your home at too low a price can negatively affect the asking price that other potential homebuyers want to make to future sellers.

These ripple effects are the same in HOA communities. An HOA owner who doesn't take care of their property, like their windows, or who hangs clothing in a visible area, can have their home appear rundown. The Grievance or Fining Committee can fine the owner for this type of neglect.

If you are a condo owner who wishes to sell your unit, that selling price can be negatively affected if the property is improperly maintained or where there is little to no compliance with rules. In such cases, some owners would have a mini zoo in their units. There can be fights over elevators during move-ins and move-outs. Furniture deliveries can take place at all hours of the day and night. Owners can have construction work done without a permit and without regard to normal working hours. In short, these condos eventually become short term rental havens.

Guests who overstay their welcome can potentially become permanent fixtures and present another problem to your lovely condo, your beautiful HOA home, or your perfect single-family. According to www.zumper.com, states within the country vary between the number of days (14- 30), as to when a visitor becomes a "tenant". The time limit for your guest, set by your board, HOA, or city, is for your own well-being and to preclude your having to eventually pay to evict them. Research the policies for your city.

The takeaway here is that as an owner of one of these types of homes, your actions, from maintaining your property inside and out, to being considerate of your community, matter. Many rules really do preserve the value and integrity of your home.

Chapter 13:
Breakdown of The Boards

Throughout my years in this industry, many owners have expressed that most board members are unfit to run a million-dollar corporation because they have no idea how to. This may be true or appear to be so for different reasons. On one hand, some owners cannot run for the board because either their accounts are delinquent at the time of elections, or they have a criminal background which excludes them from doing so. For whatever the reason, some of these individuals attempt to cause chaos for the board by delaying important matters from going forward, or by outright violating association guidelines.

On the other hand, there are those owners who wait for the board of directors and/or management to make an error so they can report them to the Department of Business and Professional Regulation **(DBPR),** or their state's equivalent. In which case, they attempt to collect money from the board as restitution for the errors made against them. This is just one reason I insist owners carefully read rules and by-laws for their associations. You want to have a realistic expectation of what your particular board and management should and can do for you.

It's counterproductive to pay lawsuits from association funds because all owners will feel the adverse effect of the disbursed funds. At the same time, when owners try to get money from the insurance, premiums tend to increase or get canceled, depending on how many pending lawsuits there are. Owners are advised to consult the association's attorney about other lawsuits, and possible alternatives to resolving major issues.

The complaint that some board members serve to further their personal agendas and are unconcerned about the needs of the majority is common. That they want rules to benefit them and their friends, or to have a sense of control over others, is another popular opinion. Read the responsibilities and structure of the different boards to get an idea of your rights as an investor if you are unhappy with your representatives.

Responsibilities of HOA Board of Directors:

- The BOD chooses a property management company to ensure owners adhere to the rules and regulations.

- The elected officers (positions vary per association) communicate with the property management company concerning the replacement, repair, and maintenance of common areas.

- To ensure all common area bills are paid on a timely basis, two board members are required to sign off on checks written on behalf of the association. These members should be clearly known to all members.

- Creates an estimated budget with the management for daily maintenance and future projects.

- Determines if and the length of time a special assessment is needed to cover additional expenses for large projects.
- Instructs management on fees for services to owners.
- Cooperates with management on miscellaneous issues: move-ins, owner complaints, etc.
- Issues violations to owners through a Grievance or Fining Committee

Structure of HOA Board of Directors:

- Consists of directors and officers over 18 years old with no criminal background.
- The number of directors and officers vary depending on the governing docs of the association.
- Elected by homeowners in good standing.
- Elected board members vote for officers to fill positions as President, Vice President, Secretary and Treasurer.
- President sets agenda, Secretary handles minutes & the Treasurer reviews monthly finances with management.
- Officers' and board members' obligations are outlined in HOA by-laws, which vary.

It's essential to know the backgrounds (especially if they have related business experience) of the candidates you choose to represent you on the board. Once you select them to represent you, they become directors and therefore difficult to remove. Do the necessary research to understand the procedures to remove either the director or officer if they are not representing your investment to your satisfaction. But you will need a certain number of investors to agree first.

As of this publication, board members can serve no more than eight consecutive years unless no one else wants to run for the board. This time limit varies by state. As an investor, you want fresh pairs of eyes and new ideas to manage your investment.

The authoritative documents for HOAs are the Declaration of Covenants, Conditions and Restrictions, or the CC&R and the by-laws.

Duties of Condo Board of Directors:

Responsibilities closely resemble those of HOA board of directors.

Structure of Condo Board of Directors:

- Directors are elected by homeowners who are not delinquent, at least 18 years of age, and have passed a background check. The number of directors varies depending on the governing docs of that condo.

- Officers consist of the President, Vice President, Secretary and Treasurer who are chosen by their peers.

- The President has the same rights as other members.

- Board members and executives make motions and vote on them.
- Specific condo by-laws explain the duties of boards and officers.
- Directors are subject to removal by the majority vote of board members.
- Officers can be removed by a specified percentage vote of the association.

Whether boards represent a condo or HOA, they exist to meet the interests of the investors/owners who elect them and to do so with integrity. Both board members and owners are responsible for knowing and following the by-laws, and to cooperate to make the best of the ownership experience.

Chapter 14:
Maybe You'd Rather Buy a Home in an HOA

Now that you have read the chapters which outline the steps to purchasing a condominium and home in an HOA, let me give you an idea of the rules and regulations for living in an HOA. Most HOA rules share commonalities with condos, although each association has guidelines that are specific to their community. Here is a list of rules however, that can differ from those of a condo:

- Restricts parking on your own lawn even for a special event.

- No recreational or commercial vehicles allowed.

- Has guidelines for trash placement /recycling.

- Pet size and pet type restrictions, anti- nuisance ordinances, and possible pet removal from the community.

- Requires a series of permits and licenses for the association's architectural committee and county officials to be provided throughout every stage of a job. Requires permits before an owner can make external changes to their property.

- Strict rules on the payment of fines and maintenance fees to avoid collections and possible foreclosure.

- Violations imposed for noncompliance with noise time limits.
- Hurricane shutters, property signs, & exterior holiday decorations subject to HOA guidelines.
- There are certain rules about holiday decorations you will have to follow.

Like the rules and regulations of condos, those above are designed to protect the property values of the homeowners' investment.

Which Home Is for You?

Quick Comparative View Of Single-Family Residence Ownership

Categories Condo HOA Home Non HOA Home

	Condo	HOA Home	Non HOA Home
Professionals needed for purchasing process	Realtor, real estate lawyer, title company, inspector(s), property management, appraiser, mortgage lender	Same as condo	All are the same, except there is no property manager. Some homeowners of all types, choose to sell their homes without a realtor
Buyer background checks	Criminal, credit, employment	Criminal, credit, employment	Employment, credit
Supervisory /management bodies	Association board of directors, officers, property management	Association board of directors, officers, property management	City, county, state enforcement
Rules & Regulations	Created by the developer for the board to oversee	Same as condo	City, county, state ordinances
Monthly Payments	Mortgage, taxes, maintenance fees & possible special assessment	Same as condo	Mortgage including related taxes, Internet, utilities, water, PMI (private mortgage insurance – time length varies) are additional.
Investigations before closing:	Tax liens, flood zone, violations, surveys, buyer loan approval	Same as condo	Same
Violations	Board fining or Grievance Committee issues violations & terms for resolution of violations	Same as condo	Codes enforcement issue violations on behalf of county, city, state
Owner responsibilities	Secures board approved certified vendors for repairs, replacements, warranties for appliances & maintenance of individual units. Work must be board approved	Same as condo	Owner responsible for daily maintenance of exterior: lawn, snow removal. Owner determines & secures all repairs, replacements, renovations, appliances, & locates vendors. Certain property renovations require county permits & related policies

This chart offers a glimpse of the basic similarities and differences of home buying and ownership for the three types of properties covered in this book.

Chapter 15:
Maybe You'd Prefer a Single Family Home

I have provided more details about the condo /HOA experience and about those areas that owners find the most challenging. The chart in the previous chapter offers a very basic comparison of the 3 types of single-family ownerships. I'll spend a few moments sharing a few points about single family dwellings in non-HOAs. None of these chapters is meant to give you a full explanation of its title, but a working reference.

Buying into an HOA home or condo is about a potential owner investing into a community, its financial condition and its regulations. A person must view conforming to this entity as necessary for the protection and increased value of their investment.

Buying into a single-family non-HOA home is also an investment, especially as home prices are expensive. Here, a potential owner invests in an entire neighborhood where the surrounding homes and businesses, school district (school taxes can be factored in the mortgage), local transportation, and other infrastructure are weighed in the purchase. While most of the same professionals are needed for the title and violations search, the buying and selling process, and most of the documents are similar, there are some lifestyle factors that can move buyers toward non-HOA ownership:

- No pet restrictions (of course neighbors can have a problem with unruly pets and their waste).

- No restrictions on guests and visiting time (though owners should be mindful of being stuck with non-rent paying "tenants")

- If you purchase a single-family home, you have a better opportunity to sell your home at a higher price.

- Usually, no special assessment fees. However, there are certain occasions when a special assessment is needed to repair a sidewalk, for example, which will be included in the property taxes.

- Street parking rules are determined by the county.

- The county or other local bodies issue warnings if an owner violates certain ordinances like noise or the proper permits for renovations.

- Neighborhoods with an active block or community association can set the tone of a neighborhood and your autonomy over your exterior.

Thorough inspections of all the working aspects of a home are essential for this type of home purchase. I suggest that shoppers investigate an entire neighborhood at different times of the day to see and feel what it's like, and to get a sense of what's happening on the block. Carefully look into police reports, criminal complaints, neighbors' feedback and school district performance, if you are looking for a neighborhood in which to raise children.

Chapter 16:
Other Tips

Reminder, I am not an attorney. The information I'm sharing with you is based on what I have learned as a professional in this industry. I attended seminars, watched videos, and spoke with experts on these subjects as part of my research. I encourage you to further investigate what I have presented. I have shared with you information I will give my own daughter when she is ready to decide on the home that is best for her.

Shopping Around

- Condos are best bought if they are between 5 - 30 years old. See Chapter 8.

- Select a realtor who has sold at least ten condominiums and is experienced in obtaining the documents, inspectors, and other professionals you will need to advance the sale.

- Check out properties of interest at various times during the day and get feedback from a variety of sources about life there.

- Make sure all **amenities** (pool, clubhouse, fitness center, etc.) listed in the condo /HOA description are available and working.

- Research the condo and HOA property management companies. DO NOT rely solely on search engine results, as

- the reviews can be one-sided. More people usually complain rather than praise the work a property management does. Visit the office 2 to 3 separate times to get varied resident feedback on the property management company and on how the board manages money.

- It's best to not purchase a condo or into an HOA in the middle to end of December. This is when budget season usually occurs, and there is a possibility maintenance fees may increase and/or when a special assessment could be created for the new year.

Inspections / Appraisals

You should have your home inspection done 15 days before purchasing the property. I suggest you get two property inspections, although some loan providers only allow one appraisal submission.

- There are two types of home inspections: One is called a **four-point inspection** which is mainly for the insurance underwriter to evaluate the level of risk to insure the property. This inspection only inspects the roof and structure, plumbing, electrical, and HVAC system.

- A **full inspection** gives you the complete condition of that home from the exterior, interior, appliances, structural integrity, as well as plumbing/ water leaks. Have a full inspection done to know how much money you will need to cough up shortly after you have purchased your home. You want to minimize financial surprises.

- An appraisal advises you of the market value of your potential home considering lot size, home condition, values of comparable homes and school zones.

- Even if the sale falls through, the buyer still pays the appraisal fee.

- Inquire if the seller has ever had an issue with mold. If yes, find out when and how the issue was addressed. Note also that not every black spot in an area is a sign of mold.

Finances

- Research any special home buying, home loan programs you may be eligible for as a first-time buyer, because of your veteran or income status /credit score. For example, if the property is FHA - Federal Housing Administration approved, they insure it and can garner an FHA approved loan for lower to moderate income borrowers. Check if an association has a credit score requirement for ownership.

- Be honest with yourself and your realtor about the home you can afford at the time of your search.

- No matter the type of home you purchase, go into it with at least $5,000 - $10,000 or more in preparation for emergencies and unexpected repairs.

- Purchase an **H06** insurance policy, which covers liability, damages, and belongings within your unit, if for some reason you are unable to live in your condo due to a covered incident. This type of policy covers what the condo common area insurance will not.

- Know and understand what your insurance policy covers before an emergency arises.

- All 3 property owners are required to pay property taxes. For example, after local governments in Florida determine their annual budgets, the county tax collectors mail tax bills to homeowners at the end of October through the first part of November. The owner is then responsible to pay their taxes before March 31st. If you are a New York City homeowner, you have the option to pay property taxes two or four times a year, depending on the property's assessed value. The amount due is posted on the NYC website at least 1 month before your taxes are due.

- Once you have closed on your condo or home in an HOA, it's imperative to provide the association with a copy of the Warranty Deed and HUD, so management can establish your account as the owner.

- Remember the home buying process is never the same for any two people. There are different scenarios when a purchase is made by cash, FHA loan, or a conventional loan. Individuals may have a certain debt ratio as well as different assets. Therefore, I urge anyone intending to purchase a home to seek expert advice from the professionals listed in the chart in Chapter 14.

Owner Involvement

- As a homeowner of a (HOA) you should be involved in one or more committees such as (architectural, landscaping, budgeting or social). You are investing in your home and in the common areas connected to it. By attending BOD meetings, you have a chance to hear what motions are being passed.

- Be familiar with the background clearance and other requirements for eligibility to serve on the board.

- You should hold your Board of Directors to a high standard. When they signed off on the Rules and Regulations, they also certified that they watched the required Board of Directors video, (If required by your state) and all governing related documents. Their signature confirms they will adhere to them.

Please keep in mind the BOD members are volunteers who have chosen to protect your investment and theirs. It's for your protection to read more than their **curriculum vitae** about their background before you allow them to represent you. You should ask each candidate specific questions as to how they will represent you and care for your investment. Be convinced that they will listen to your concerns and be transparent to explain how they arrived at their decisions. At the end of the day, you as the investor, are choosing someone to fulfill their fiduciary duties, which are not to steal, commit any criminal activities, or to get **kickbacks**.

- A homeowner who is elected to the Board must complete a certification course within 90 days (about 3 months) of being elected or appointed. In the event someone has not completed the course, they are to submit a letter to the Secretary stating they have read all the governing documents and will uphold them, as well as comply with the fiduciary responsibilities to all homeowners. (May vary by state.)

- As a homeowner in an association, you want to attend board meetings to make sure the board fairly enforces the rules and regulations. In addition, you want to confirm that they communicate transparently with all homeowners and act in good faith to address the needs of the entire association.

- Once you buy a condo or into an HOA, I suggest that you read the last five to ten board meeting minutes to understand their vision to maintain the property and the association. As a homeowner, you should either read or listen to the audiobook of Robert's Rules Of Order by Henry M. Robert III. This will give you a clearer understanding of the order and decency with which the board of directors should manage your investment.

Rules

- The association should not be able to enforce a rule contradicted by its declaration. Although a board may propose a rule that changes or modifies the declaration, it still needs the owners' votes to approve the change and to follow the procedures for amending that declaration. The board may not act alone in this regard.

- Associations without **Grievance Committees** will be challenged to collect fines when an owner/tenant/resident breaks the rules and regulations. The association must have an active Grievance Committee consisting of individual owners who are not on or are related to the board of directors. Check your highest document to see if this applies to your condo.

- It's important for potential buyers to review the declaration of the condo or HOA board. Just because the board proposed a rule that has not been approved by the membership, doesn't mean it must be followed without amendment. Read your documents to understand what your board can and cannot do.

- Be familiar with the board and owners' voting rights.

- If you don't wish to be a part of the condominium registry, you should request a form that states your information only be used for accounting and condominium business.

- The master deed or CC&Rs (Covenants, Conditions, and Restrictions) is regulated by the Condominium Act and will be recorded in the public records of the county where the property is located.

- Board members should operate association business moderately. They should not seek out cheap materials, poor service, or practice extravagant spending.

- As an HOA owner you will need to seek approval from the BOD to update the exterior of your home. There are some HOAs that require you to obtain approval to make certain changes inside your home. Refer to your association architectural modification process.

Chapter 17:
BONUS CHAPTER: Real Life Stories

I have included two home purchase scenarios. The first is a family's experience with an HOA home purchase in their own words, starting in April 2021 until their closing at the end of June 2021. I felt it was essential for you to be aware of their step-by-step process, and the violation that occurred within two weeks of their move-in. The second is one couple's experience which became a lengthy ordeal.

In the first week of April 2021, we met with a realtor and told her how many rooms we were looking for and the location we wanted to move into. Within days, the realtor set us up to meet with a loan officer. Once we met with the loan officer, we were required to provide that person with the following documents: 3 months' pay stubs, 3 months of bank statements, 401K information, credit card information, W2, and proof that we paid our rent-on time. We were also advised not to spend excessively during this time.

A few weeks later, we were told the amount we qualified for, and we then started searching on a particular realtor's website. We narrowed down a few houses in HOAs and had our realtor show them to us. Our realtor worked on submitting contracts while we waited to hear if a seller accepted our offer. During this time, we both received raises which we informed the loan officer about.

During this process, we were asked several times to submit the same documents repeatedly to the loan officer. Once the contract was accepted, we heard from the title company, who told us how much we needed to put in escrow for the closing. Also, during this time, the HOA sent us a 250-page book about the association we were required to read.

We then set up appointments for the home inspectors and appraiser, which we attended. According to the contract, we had to pay for both appointments. Once the inspection reports came back, the realtor said the title company would send information on wiring the money into escrow. A week later, we were provided with our closing date and instructed where and when to wire the down payment.

On the day of closing, we met with our realtor, and the seller and their realtor, and did the last walk-through in the house. Thereafter, the sellers and their realtors went to the title company to sign the documents. Once the seller executed all the documents, we went in and signed our portion.

We met with the board of directors the day after the closing who had received our documents from the title company. The day we moved in, our neighbor saw that our grass was a little too high and he went ahead and cut it for us. We found that gesture to be so nice and helpful to avoid a violation we could have received.

One week later, we received a violation. My husband, in his rush to work, pulled the garbage pail out of the garage and left it in front of the garage door. The HOA rules require that bins be placed at the edge of the sidewalk in front of the house. We had to sign and date a letter stating we would place the garbage in the proper area from then on. My husband and I will be reading the rules and regulations more closely to make sure we become familiar with all of them.

Here is another play-by-play of a recent single family home purchase shared with me by a couple of young newlyweds. I can't say everyone will go through the exact process, but the steps will be similar.

The couple contacted a family friend, who was also a realtor, to start the process of purchasing a single-family home. When the realtor spoke with them, they were told they should pay off a few bills to increase their credit score. They followed the suggestion and submitted a formal letter to end their lease before they had a home to move into. They walked by faith and not by sight. They trusted that God would provide one for them even though they had no contract signed for a new home in sight. A family member opened their home to them so they could have peace of mind while they went through the process.

The pre-approved process went smoothly. All the documents the lender requested were submitted, and within a week they were provided with the amount they were pre-approved to spend. Although they received their pre-approved dollar amount, they agreed to purchase a home for considerably less than that amount. They also agreed this first home would eventually become a rental property. They agreed to have only one name on the loan, with both names on the deed. This way, when they were ready to rent this property, both names would not be tied up and responsible for the loan.

They made an offer on the first home they saw because it was near family and in an excellent location. The offer wasn't accepted but they were okay with the decision. Their attitude was no one could take away the home God had for them.

A week later their realtor contacted them to see a home another couple had just passed up. Although it wasn't within their ideal budget and larger than their preferred size, the realtor asked if they would be open to seeing the property. Once they saw the home, they made an offer above the asking price. Thirty minutes later the offer was accepted, but with stipulations. The seller wanted $6000.00 earnest money as proof the buyers were serious. They instead offered $5000.00 earnest money, which the seller accepted.

The following day they scheduled an inspection of the home which revealed minor repairs that needed taking care of, which the seller agreed to do before closing. They went into the **underwriting** process and then into the appraisal. (To understand the underwriting and the appraisal process go to www.rocketmortgage.com/learn/what-is-underwriting).

During this process however, the city code violations notified the seller, who requested additional time to address the outstanding violations. The appraisal was given, but at a lower price than the seller and buyer expected. The seller had put many upgrades into the home, but the appraisal didn't allow her to recoup the funds used for the improvements. There wasn't much the couple could do because they had taken out an FHA loan and that company would not accept a reappraisal.

What the buyers initially thought would be a timely closing turned out to be a process that dragged on for weeks. The seller stalled on the repairs and had the home reappraised after the house next door was sold. After several addendums, more communications, and some re-negotiations among all the parties, the buyers eventually closed on the deal. At one point they seriously considered scrapping their offer altogether, until their attorney reminded them to hang in there as they were in the midst of a seller's market.

Major plumbing and A/C issues also arose after their move-in, with the discovery that the A/C had never been properly ventilated. They wondered why none of this was brought to their attention during the inspections. Some buyers choose to use more than one inspector to compare reports and avoid this outcome but be prepared that this can be expensive.

This couple recommends that if anyone is not buying a completely brand-new home for the first time, they must ALWAYS have an **emergency fund.** They like the idea of their own space, but had they known better, they would have remained renters until they had sufficient "just in case" funds to cover any problem. The upside is that they believe homeownership means they have equity in their home, and that it is theirs to do as they choose within limits. At the time of this publication, the violations on the property were still pending. The couple anxiously toddles around the house waiting for things to break.

Acknowledgements and Credits

I want to start by thanking my daughter, Jasmin Lewis Pierre, a graduate of Jiangsu Normal University, China. She encouraged me to finish this book despite the many times I stopped. Next, I want to acknowledge my friend, Jimmy V., who encouraged me to utilize the passion he saw when we worked together in this industry.

I must thank all the prior and current property owners who submitted survey responses. I am grateful to Jamel Spalding (Yummo Bucko-food vlogger), for the many nights he encouraged his viewers to pursue whatever passion they had, no matter what.

To my other group of friends who encouraged me along the way by asking if I was finished, because they wanted to support me and get a signed copy, FRIENDS, you know who you are, for it's a small circle: Princess Nikki B and Kenya Stevens. Thank you!

I can't forget to thank those known by the initials, A.A and J.G., who were an immense help to me during this process by allowing me to bounce my book ideas off them. Special mention to Adrian Gray of Intamax Marketing for his proofreading, editing and revision services. Also for the information provided concerning the electric vehicles and questions that should be asked. Finally, I can't forget to thank Mr. & Mrs. Ellington and Mr. & Mrs. Jean Baptiste for sharing their purchasing process journey with me. I would like to thank one of God's vessels, Patricia Gordon of WORD SANCTUARY, LLC for her editing services.

Thank you so much for allowing me to share information along with my experiences. I hope the research I have done to help my daughter also helps you to decide which home is best for you. Whether you call this a book or a guide, I hope it encourages you to make the right decision on purchasing a home. I am satisfied knowing that I have shared my knowledge related to home buying and ownership that you might not have known existed, and which you now have a better understanding of.

Glossary

718.116(11) Florida Statutes on renting your unit

1. ACH- Automated Clearing House

2. Amenities- A useful or desirable feature or facility that can be included in a property purchase. They are also communal areas: pool, gym, sauna, clubhouse, or tennis court.

3. Approved Budget- Is a projection of the money the association needs to cover its operating expenses. It also gives potential owners an idea of the estimated expenses they will be responsible for by owning in that association.

4. Assigned parking spaces- Parking spaces that are designated by the association but which the owner does not have exclusive rights to. The declaration indicates who and how they may control the parking space.

5. AutoPay- This is one of the best ways for an owner to pay monthly fees and to avoid late fees.

6. By-laws- Guidelines for individuals who reside in a condominium association and which they agree to comply with to avoid receiving violations.

7. Charging Station- A location designated on the property in the common area where electronic vehicles are charged.

8. **ClickPay** as per clickpayclientsupport.zendesk.com - Is a payment solution that automates the entire billing and receivables process, collects all forms of payments, and

provides real-time business insights and management reporting.

9. Collections in relation to an association home – Is when an attorney is hired to collect an outstanding amount owed for maintenance and or special assessment. A single-family homeowner will deal directly with the bank concerning their unpaid mortgage.

10. Common elements - The shared areas of an association, e.g., parking area (garage), driveways, swimming pool, elevators, or clubhouse.

11. Condominium Association- As per https://kmlegal.com - Each member owns their individual unit, and they have joint ownership/interest in the communal areas.

12. Coupon Booklets - 12 condo payment coupons for each monthly payment of the year.

13. Curriculum Vitae – A summary of education and professional achievements that candidates who run for the board of an association will submit with their application.

14. DBPR Department Of Business and Professional Regulation - Oversees the regulations of licensed business professionals in Florida.

15. Declaration Of the Condominium- Is the highest document for an association. It describes the maintenance requirements and the common elements.

16. Deeded Parking Space- An owner actually owns the parking space and not the association. For more details concerning deeded parking space you can go to: https://askmistercondo.com/deeded-parking .

17. Earnest Money – As per homebuyer.com, this is the up-front amount a buyer pays as a down payment as proof of their commitment to buy the property.

18. Emergency Fund - Money that is saved and put aside for situations such as major home repairs.

19. Escrow – As per homebuyer.com, a "savings" account managed by a buyer's mortgage servicer, law firm, title company, or escrow company. The escrow provider safeguards the funds and protects all parties by ensuring that the terms of the purchase contract and mortgage agreement are carried out.

20. ESA - An emotional support animal that provides comfort to help relieve a symptom or effect of a person's disability. This animal is not considered a pet.

21. Estimated Close Date - Is the anticipated date agreed upon by the seller and buyer to close the purchase deal. The closing can happen before the date mentioned, but not after the agreed date, unless the contract is amended to reflect the new date.

22. Estoppel - A document that shows if the current owner has an outstanding balance in maintenance and/or special

assessment fees. To read more details concerning Estoppels go to www.floridarealtors.org.

23. EVs- Electric vehicles

24. FHA - U.S. Federal Housing Administration mortgage insurance backed by an FHA-approved lender. This is an insured loan which is a type of federal assistance. This type of loan allows lower-income Americans to borrow and purchase a home they would otherwise not be able to afford.

25. First Right of Refusal - This applies to associations' closings. As per their by-laws, most associations have the right to purchase a unit from the owner first before an outside buyer may do so.

26. Fiduciary responsibility- The person or persons (board of directors) who is acting on behalf of the owners' financial interest.

27. Flood Insurance as per www.investopedia - Insurance that covers a dwelling for losses sustained by water damage specifically due to flooding. For more details, the site will explain this insurance in more detail.

28. Floor Plan - A diagram of a unit's walls and room layout which cannot be changed without the condo or HOA's approval. The approval is needed to make sure the structure of the unit or building will not be damaged, and cause issues to arise.

Glossary

29. Four Point Inspection as per rocketmortgage.com - A 4-point inspection is an examination of the current condition of a house or condominium reviewing four major systems: roofing, electrical, plumbing, and HVAC.

30. Full Inspection as per berylprojectengineering.com - A comprehensive examination that focuses on heating and cooling systems, efficiency and potential issues, appliances inside the house, plumbing problems, basement and crawlspace, roof, chimney and fireplace, electrical system including breakers and receptacles, structural integrity, and condition of the interior and exterior surface.

31. Grievance Committee - A group of owners who are not on the board of directors, and who are unrelated to members of the board. They review violations committed by owners or tenants in the association. If you want further information pertaining to the state of Florida, see section 720.305, Florida Statutes or seek legal counsel.

32. HUD Housing Urban Development - As per www.hud.gov, HUD helps to create a decent home and suitable living environment for all Americans, and it has given America's communities a strong national voice at the Cabinet level. HUD plays a key role in supporting homeownership by underwriting homeownership for lower- and moderate-income families through its mortgage insurance programs.

33. HOA Homeowners Association as per https://kmlegal.com - Each member owns their individual property and their lot.

The communal areas are owned by the Homeowner's association.

34. H06 Insurance Policy www.progressive.com - Sometimes referred to as "H06 Insurance," can cover liability claims, damage to an owner's condo unit and belongings, and additional living expenses, should the condo become unlivable.

35. Kickbacks - Payments made to a board member, managers, or others who make and/or influence decision making for an association, in return for an illicit transaction.

36. LCAM (Licensed Community Association Manager) - An individual licensed to handle the day-to-day operations of an association.

37. Lien - A legal claim on assets that allows the holder to obtain access to the property if the outstanding debt is not paid.

38. Litigation cases - Lawsuits in which a party is seeking damages for a wrong or neglect.

39. Maintenance - A monthly fee owners pay to cover the expenses for the common area/amenities that they use. This fee will increase usually once a year. The BOD approves this fee.

40. Noise Ordinance as per www.legalmatch.com - A local law which prohibits excessive and unnecessary noise. Ordinances often include prohibitions on excessive noise during certain hours.

Glossary

41. Notarized document- The said document is legally considered authentic and sealed by a notary public.

42. Notice of Commencement - Document which states the start date of a project for which a vendor is performing their services, or the date when the vendor provided supplies or labor. This document is recorded in the county of the state the association is located in.

43. Premium as per www.policygenius.com - Is the amount a policy holder pays every year to keep their policy active. Insurance premiums are generally paid in one of two ways: either directly to the insurance company with one-time or recurring payments, or as part of an owner's monthly mortgage payment.

44. Preapproved or (Prequalified) - As per Consumer Financial Protection Bureau, both terms mean that a lender is willing to lend a potential buyer a certain amount of money, if the financial info provided is verified, and if a deeper dive into financials does not raise any red flags.

45. Purchase Agreement as per https://www.rocketmortgage.com - A legally binding agreement that governs the purchase and sale of a property. Made between a buyer and seller, it defines the terms of the transaction, and the conditions under which a sale will occur.

46. Quitclaim Deed – A legal document a seller transfers to a buyer, but which does not guarantee ownership of the title of the property being sold to that buyer.

47. Reservations- The specific date and time that owners and tenants in a condo contact management to schedule the elevator for a delivery, move-in, or move-out.

48. Reserve Budget – As per reservebudgets.com, this budget gives those overseeing the maintenance of a property a better idea of what major expenses to expect, and an educated estimate of when these expenses will occur.

49. Reserve Study - A budget planning tool which observes the funds that have been collected up until a particular time for the items in question. A funding plan is then put into place to offset the ongoing items.

50. Rules and Regulations - Governs the associations and are created by the board of directors to enforce upon owners, tenants, and guests to keep the community running harmoniously.

51. Single- family home - A home that sits on its own parcel of land and is not part of an association.

52. Special Assessment - As per Florida 718.404, is an assessment levied against a unit owner in addition to the assessment required by a budget adopted annually. When the association has not collected enough funds to pay for major projects not addressed in the approved budget, an additional fund collection becomes necessary.

53. Sufficient Funds Affidavit -This document indicates that the association has the funds on hand to pay for work it is

about to do, or which is already in progress. This then leads to the **Notice of Commencement.**

54. Underwriting- Verifies your income, assets, debts, and property details to suggest the amount of risk a mortgage lender will take if they decide to give you a loan.

55. Violations – An act or condition not permissible for a property owner or tenant. 718.303 is a statute in Florida that controls how a condominium imposes fines against owners, tenants, guests etc. Look up 730.305, the statute in Florida that controls how an HOA imposes fines against owners, tenants, guests, etc. Read and understand the details in understanding code violations concerning Single Family Homes in Devon Thorsby's report on *Common Housing Code Violations and Questions to Ask About Them.*

56. Warranty Deed- The seller confirms legal ownership of a property, with no outstanding liens or mortgages that could grant an outside party the right to the property once a buyer owns it.

57. Warranty- A written guarantee that the seller of goods or property presents to a buyer to repair or replace defects found in the item or property, during a specified period.

58. Wind Mitigation- Inspections performed in the state of Florida by a licensed building contractor or certified architect which costs between $100 to $150.00. It confirms that shingles meet the Florida building code requirements for homes built before March 1, 2002.

Links:

40-year recertification information regarding lights

https://www.darkskysociety.org

www.broward.org

www.ingramcontent.com/pod-product-compliance
Lightning Source LLC
Chambersburg PA
CBHW051051230426
43666CB00012B/2653